MARTIN LUTHER

THINKER REBEL MONK

THE HISTORY HOUR

HISTORY

CONTENTS

TIMELINE OF IMPORTANT EVENTS IN LUTHER'S LIFE

To be a Christian without prayer is no more possible than to be alive without breathing.
Martin Luther

❧

1483
On 10th of November, Martin Luther is born in Eisleben, Saxony to Hans and Margrethe Luder

❧

1484
Luther's family moves to Mansfeld where his father holds several copper mines on lease

❧

1492

Luther's father Hans Luder is elected town councilor

❦

1497-1498

Luther is sent to a Latin school in Madgeburg and then
Eisenach

❦

1501-1505

At age 17, Luther enrolls at University of Erfurt and four years
later graduates from the University with a Master's Degree

❦

1505

Luther commences his legal training as per his father's
wishes. However, finds himself more attracted to Philosophy
and Theology

❦

1505

In July Luther witnesses a Near Death Experience during a
snow storm

❦

1507

Luther is ordained by Jerome Schultz, Bishop of Brandenburg

❦

1508

Von Saupitz, who was then the Dean of the University of
Wittenburg invites Luther to teach Theology at the
university

❧

1509

Luther receives his Bachelor's degree in Sentences

❧

1512

Luther is awarded Doctor of Theology and joins the Senate
of the Theological Faculty at the University of Wittenberg

❧

1510-1511

Luther takes a break from education and serves in Rome as a
representative of the German Augustinian Monasteries

❧

1512- end of his career

Luther rightly succeeded Saupitz and remained the Chair of
Theology at the university until the very end of his career.

❧

1515

Luther was finally made the Provincial Vicar of Saxony with a
dozen monasteries under his care

※

1512-1517

Luther immersed himself into a deep study of Christian Theology

※

1517

Luther writes the *95 Theses Disputation on The Power and Efficacy of Indulgences* in response to the practice of selling indulgences. They are published in Leipez and Basel.

※

1518

The Pope officially declares Luther's writings conflicting with the Church

※

1520

The Papal Bull declared Luther a heretic with 120 days to recant

※

1521

Diet of Worms takes place and Philip 1 meets Luther while Luther refuses to recant for his teachings

※

1521

Pope Leo excommunicated Luther, who goes into hiding as he is declared a convict and his writings are banned and burnt

❦

1521-1522

Luther goes into hiding first in Wartburg and then Eisenach and returns in 1522

❦

1523

Luther writes *Jesus was born a Jew*

❦

1524

Philip 1 embraces Protestantism at the hands of Melanchthon and aides the protestant Reformation through power and wealth

❦

1525

Luther marries Katharina Von Bora, an escapee of a convent in Nimbsch

❦

1526

First Imperial Diet of Spires is held and ensured protestants and local German rulers more autonomy regarding reformation

❧

1527

Luther writes the devotional song *A Mighty Fortress in our Lord*

❧

1528

Philipp Melanchthon writes *Instruction on the Visitations to Pastors in the Electorate of Saxon* and receives Luther's approval

❧

1528

Luther averts a sectarian religious war by calling for peace and tolerance

❧

1529

Luther established the *Small and Large Catechism, Smart Song Book* and *Wedding Book*

❧

1529

Luther takes six of his sister's children into his modest home

❧

1530

The Imperial Diet of Augsburg forbade all reform actions, prompted Melanchthon to write Augsburg Confession-detailing beliefs of reformists

❦

1530
Smalkaldian alliance is formed to protect Protestants from Catholic attacks.

❦

1531-1536
Luther begins experiencing ill health, eye and ear infections and what would later develop into kidney and gall bladder stones.

❦

1533-1546
Luther serves his term as the Dean of Theology at the University of Wittenberg

❦

1542
Luther loses his daughter Magdelina

❦

1543
Luther writes *Jews and their Lies*

❦

1545-1546
Luther occupies himself with arbitrating disputes between Mansfeld counts

❧

1545

Luther writes *Against the Papacy at Rome Founded by the Devil*

❧

1546

Luther delivers his last sermon Eisleben which is heavily against the Jews and calls for their removal.

❧

1546

On the 18th of February, Luther dies in Eisleben and is laid to rest in Castle Church on 22nd February.

❧

1546-1547

The Schmalkaldic war takes place to suppress protestants

❧

1548

King Charles forces Protestants and Schmalkadic league to submit to the terms of Augsburd interim

❧

1555

Holy Roman Empire finally recognizes Protestantism as a legitimate religious denomination within the empire.

✣ II ✣

INTRODUCTION

꧁꧂

Let the wife make the husband glad to come home,
and let him make her sorry to see him leave.
   Martin Luther

꧁꧂

Martin Luther (1483-1546) can be regarded as one of the most
prominent thinkers of the Christian world since St. Augustine and St. Aquinas. Armed by intellect and logic and a fiery
passion to stand up against injustice and untruth, this man
single handedly took the Western world by storm in the 16th
century. What put him in the spotlight were not just his
novel ideas that had never been entertained by the Church
before, but also his actions which were fearless and his
courage and firm resolve to see his mission through.

While the name Martin Luther might evoke a somewhat mixed response from the global community, with many confusing him with his more modern name-sake, Dr. Martin Luther King Jr., in the Christian world his name bears an unmistakable distinction. Most famous as the father of Lutheranism; a vibrant strain of Christian enquiry, reform and reconciliation through the ages; the great thinker was able to change History, at least how Christianity has experienced it, through his unending quest for the truth and his unwavering support to what he regarded as the right cause.

As a thinker whose thoughts shaped Christianity through the last part of the 15th and beginning of the 16th century and became an inspiration for reformers for centuries to come, it is interesting to study the life of this great man and in doing so come face to face with his personality, achievements and the ideals he stood for. The more we study him the more we realize that most of his concerns and ideals were timeless, and a lot like concerns we share today. Thus, though detached from him by centuries we too might find solace in the things that brought meaning to his life. More so, in order to be truly inspired by Martin Luther, we need to delve into his experiences and fish out the most profound and most actionable tips that when applied in our lives could transform us and help us achieve our true potential as human beings.

❧ III ❧

STORM IN THE DISTANCE- LUTHER'S BIRTH

❦❧

God writes the Gospel not in the Bible alone, but also on trees, and in the flowers and clouds and stars.
Martin Luther

❦❧

The fact that Luther's coming to the center stage of Church life in Germany caused a storm within Christendom, due to his unconventional ideas and unwavering support for the truth isn't hidden from anybody. He also similarly surprised his father by his oft wavering ambitions and bewildered colleagues and adversaries alike by his fearlessness and courage.

THE CHRISTIAN CHURCH
BEFORE LUTHER

❦

The Christian Church which had been based on the Catholic tradition for the most part had been thoroughly corrupted over the centuries and bore very little resemblance to the religious life and works of the disciples of Christ or the first generation of saints. By the time Luther came along, the office of the Pope in Rome had turned a blind eye to corruption and exploitation of masses that took place at the hands of Church officials, particularly in Germany. The condition of the Church before Luther was such that it had been plagued by materialism and greed for wealth to an extent that salvation was now sold for money. Moreover, while the Church had insisted that monks lead a celibate life; when the Bible never demanded celibacy; the situation within monasteries was far from noble or decent. Many a times Bishops and other priests were infamous for their licentiousness, debauchery and immoral actions. In summary, the Church had lost the love for God and his Scripture and instead of a spiritually fulfilling environ, it had created a cultist control mechanism whereby masses were misled and disempowered and manipulated for worldly gains.

LUTHER'S PARENTS AND
HOUSEHOLD

❧

L uther's father was Hans Luder or Luther, who is claimed to be of a petty peasant lineage while his mother was Margrethe Lindemann, who is sometimes defamed by being referred to as a woman of lowly manners. In which can be an attempt to ridicule Luther's background by his adversaries, some regard his father to have been a smelter, or miner at best, whereas other historical sources suggest that he was in fact a lease holder of copper mines. The latter sounds more probable as Luder ultimately got involved directly in public affairs and rose to the position of being a representative of the local citizens council and was finally elected as the town councilor. What we know about Martin Luther's mother is that she was a very hardworking woman who was extremely industrious and resourceful.

❧

WHILE LUTHER HAD SEVERAL SIBLINGS, as was customary

for families in that part of the world and that age, he was particularly close to one of his brothers- Jacob. His father had a dream of making Martin a lawyer and see him succeed materially. For this reason, he made it a point to give him the very best education.

CIRCUMSTANCES OF LUTHER'S
BIRTH AND EARLY CHILDHOOD

☙❧

Martin Luther was born to this relatively affluent and publicly active family on the 10th of November 1483 in Eisleben, Saxony which was at that time a part of the Holy Roman empire.

☙❧

In 1484, the family shifted to Mansfeld and his father provided a somewhat stable life for his family by holding several copper mines on lease. While it is not completely certain if this allowed the family to have an affluent life style, Luther's father seems to have been held in regard by the general public as is evident from his later postings in the civil services. In 1492 Luther's father was elected to be the town councilor- an honorable position. In addition to holding this influential and responsible post, the gentleman would also often take part in arbitrations and took keen interest in ensuring the peace and stability within the town.

❧

ALSO, it seems that knowing the importance and influence that a law maker could yield in German society at the time, Luther's father was prompted to give his son elite education and to train him as a lawyer to aid not only in the family's wealth and prosperity but to ensure that like himself Martin would become a prominent public figure and a man of great repute.

❧

IT MUST BE KEPT in mind that while it might seem that Luther had a relatively normal childhood with very little happening in terms of widespread violence, Germany was simmering with internal problems that were socio-economic in nature. Often these tensions poured over in the form of class wars and struggles from improvised farmers. Although major rebellions had already been crushes before Luther's birth his childhood witnessed a calm before the storm. This was the time tensions were brewing up and would finally spill over during the height of the Protestant Reformation when religious authority and legitimacy of the Church would be brought into question.

❧ IV ❧

MAKING OF A GENIUS-LUTHER'S EDUCATION AND CAREER

❦

You are not only responsible for what you say, but also for what you do not say.

Martin Luther

❦

EARLY EDUCATION

༻❀༺

I n keeping with his father's wishes to educate Martin at the very best of schools, so that he could one day train as a lawyer, he was sent to Latin schools in Mansfeld and finally in 1497 he was sent to Madgeburg. There he would study at a school operated by a group called the Brethren of Common Life and then in the following year in 1498 he was shifted to Eisenach. All the schools Luther went to focused on subjects such as grammar, rhetoric, mathematics, geometry and logic. However, the modes of instruction were so outdated and the lectures were so boring in addition to the horrid and strict teachers that in later years Luther remarked that these schools he went to were comparable to hell. This early insight into the problems that plagued German society at the grassroots level in the field of education offered young Luther an important insight into the fact that everything was not well with the way his nation viewed knowledge and education. Later in life he would question similar strictness and methodical ritualism even in the quest for Knowledge of God.

LEGAL TRAINING

৩%৪

In pursuance of his father's desire for him to pursue law, Luther enrolled for his higher education at the University of Erfurt in 1501, when he was just 17 years old. He graduated from there in 1505 with a master's degree. However, he was again disappointed with the strenuous and boring rote learning processes he had to undergo. This shows that Luther was not someone who could be forced to memorize facts without appreciating their reality and metaphysical connotations.

৩%৪

FINALLY, although he enrolled into the legal studies stream in 1505, he soon dropped out quite against his father's wishes. Luther recollects in his memoirs that it was the aspect of uncertainty that plagued the study of law which was for him a major turn off and his mind found more pleasure in studying philosophy and religion. While many believed he would have made a great lawyer given his ability to speak and convince listeners and his skills to think clearly and critically, he ultimately left the professional training to join monastic life.

꧁꧂

As for what prompted this decision of Luther's part, on one hand his heart was not into the process and on the other he had the life changing experience he had during a snow storm and had taken a vow to serve the Church if his life were spared. In the final instance, Luther decided to follow his heart and keep his vows regarding serving God as a monk.

HIGHLIGHTS OF LUTHER'S
CAREER

꧁꧂

L uther's career as a monk began once he turned to the life of a Christian recluse after his near-death experience in 1505. For the next two years he immersed himself in the worship and contemplation of God and underwent all the hardships that a monastic life demanded. In 1507 Martin Luther was ordained as a minister in the Church by Jerome Schultz, the Bishop of Brandenburg. Then, a year later in 1508 Johann Von Saupitz, who was then the Dean of the University of Wittenburg invited Luther to teach Theology at the university. Luther willingly agreed and began a legacy of teaching and learning that continued to the end of his career. This also gave him a change to build a steady base of followers among his students, who admired him greatly. These individuals would later work on to support Luther in his reformist mission and to carry on his good work after his death.

꧁꧂

AFTER HAVING SPENT 2 years teaching theology, Luther was to experience something that would change not only his career and his life but his very significance to Christian Theology and the Church forever. It was his visit to Rome that shook Luther in action and agitated his conscience to speak about against the troubling injustice, immorality, materialism and unequal treatment that he witnessed at Rome. This momentous change took place in 1510 when he had taken a year off from education so that he could serve in Rome as a representative of the German Augustinian monasteries.

❧

CONTRARY TO HIS EXPECTATIONS, Luther witnessed first-hand how there was extreme disunity among members of the church and great disparity in terms of the treatment of ministers of the Church. While some received preferential treatment, many priests like those in his group were literally harassed and treated with very little respect. The visit to Rome left Luther disillusioned about what it meant to be a part of the church or serving the papacy at Rome. In fact, such injustice and inequality made him question whether at all the Pope's office was legitimate and whether he was worthy of being the Vicar of God on earth. This sentiment would gradually develop into a full-blown rejection of the Pope's authority culminating in the publication of *Against the Papacy at Rome Founded by the Devil* in 1545.

❧

AFTER THIS BITTER and formative experience of witnessing the inner corruptions and crises within the Church the next few years from 1512 to 1517 were the most crucial in Luther's life and would serve to influence and shape many of his later revolutionary ideas that became a defining characteristic of his theological disagreements with Catholicism. Moreover, during this phase in 1514 he was appointed City Church's priest in Wittenberg. It was during these very important years that Luther immersed himself in the study of the Bible and the writings of the greatest Christian theologians like St Augustine. The insights that he gathered into theological issues during this period would serve to shake the foundations of conventional Christianity forever.

TEACHERS, CONTEMPORARIES
AND INSPIRATIONAL FIGURES

꧁꧂

A mong figures who inspired Luther after the person of Christ, Aristotle was perhaps his favorite ancient thinker and William of Ockham was one of the early Christian thinkers whom he read thoroughly. One is lead to suspect that many of his revolutionary ideas stemmed to some extend from the influence that Ockham's own revolutionary and unconventional ideas and his own struggles against headstrong clergy.

꧁꧂

LUTHER OWES a lot of debt to his two teachers who taught him at university which was otherwise an unpleasant experience for him. These great teachers, Batholomaeus Arnoldi and Jodocus Trutfether were instrumental in shaping Luther into the unrelenting revolutionary he later became. Perhaps the two greatest lessons they taught him were: to suspect what even great thinkers say and not just accept their ideas without scrutiny, and to test things for himself before actually believing in them. These two lessons instilled in him the ability to treat established wisdom with caution and to experiment and experience things first hand before wholly accepting them to be a part of reality. The impact this had on his personality is quite evident.

❦

ANOTHER MAN who entered Luther's life a lot later was Johann Von Saupitz, who held his hand during a period of great spiritual turmoil and religious disillusionment that had caused him to become utterly miserable and depressed. In his early days as a monk when Luther found himself utterly unhappy at the outwardly rituals he performed and their inability to have any inner transformative effect on his soul, Luther fell into utter despair and self-harm. It was at this point that Saupitz reassured him that this phase would soon be over. He advised him to stop focusing all his mind and energy on self-blame and punishment and instead of pitying himself to focus his attention on God, his benevolent nature and unending grace. Miraculously, this was what Luther needed and no sooner had he shifted his attention towards God's love, he found himself liberated of all the laborious outwardly rites that he had uselessly indulged in for so long in contradiction to his nature and personality.

❦

FURTHER, Luther owes a lot of gratitude to his wife, Katharina, who came into his house at a time when it was in utter ruin and disorder. While he offered her the love and security that she needed after fleeing from her earlier troubled life, she offered him the services of a good manager of his household and a strong woman who stood by him at all times.

❦

SOME CLOSE ASSOCIATES of Luther include people like Von Saupitz, George Spalatin who was a close friend, Philipp Melanchthon; who wrote about the Diet in Augsburg; Andreas Karktadt as well as Justus Jonas.

❦

MOREOVER, Luther often had intellectual exchanges with several of his contemporaries and co-religionists who voiced opinions on theology different from his own. One of his books, Bondage of Will, is regarded as a rebuttal to an earlier work, Diatribe of Freewill by Desiderius Erasmus 1524. Similarly, Luther and Johannes Agricola greatly differed with each other on the relationship between faith and deeds. While Agricola maintained that faith and deeds went hand in hand, Luther insisted that faith and works were separate from each other.

ADVERSARIES AND OPPONENTS

❦

Given his fiery nature and his unwavering stance on his unique vision of Christian theology, Martin Luther won himself more foes than friends and never had a dearth of adversaries who would love to see him dead. The Roman Catholic church was filled with priests and ministers who looked at him as if he were a heretic and devil. If they could they would have him burnt at the stake much like Joan of Arc. He is known for having a bitter association with Pope Leo and the Archbishop and Cardinal Thomas Cajetan who played an instrumental role in pushing the Pope to declare his writings as contradictory to Church doctrine. Charles V went to the extent of having all his writings burnt and the Church officials ensured that Luther was excommunicated from the Church after being declared a heretic.

❦

ALSO, one man who became a bitter enemy of Luther due to

his reform actions was the infamous priest Johann Tetzel who had been used to making money from the sale of indulgences. When Luther's 95 Theses, actually intended for academic discussion, put a dent in his pocket due to the decrease in his income, he lashed back by disapproving it and labelled Luther a heretic whom he wanted burnt at the stake.

BETWEEN THE MIND AND THE SOUL- LUTHER AS A MONK AND A THINKER

❦

Even if I knew that tomorrow the world would go to pieces, I would still plant my apple tree.

Martin Luther

❦

Luther represents a struggle of two dialectics within the nature of man: the battle between following one's mind and one's soul. While Luther had been gifted with a highly capable mind and the prowess of logical reasoning and argumentation, he did not find the fulfillment of his soul's purpose in the legal profession. He knew his heart was looking for something greater in which he could find eternal solace and love. His journey towards monastic life and the subsequent transitions that took place in his own soul made him experience the trials of faith in God firsthand and strengthened him in his devotion to the divine.

CHOOSING A MONK'S LIFE

❦

The reason Luther chose to become a monk might seem very strange to a lot of people. In Luther's case it was more like the Church chose him rather than him choosing to join the Church. From what has been often narrated, Luther's decision was not a well-calculated plan or a first step towards dismantling the Catholic church from within. Rather, it was sparked by a chance occurring during a harsh German winter. This near-death experience took place in 1505 and while he found it impossible to escape the blizzard he prayed to the saints and made a promise that he would dedicate his life to God were he to escape unhurt. Finally, when Luther did escape the storm, he had no choice but to honor his word. He therefore bid farewell to his colleagues at the university and ended his legal training on a sour note- something that didn't go very well for his father.

❦

AT THIS POINT it seems like Luther's ultimate destiny of reforming the Church had come into play and used the forces of nature to steer Luther on the path meant for him. In this way by pure chance, Luther was literally flung into the eye of the storm and subjected to some of the strictest tests of his faith and physical endurance.

જ્જ

MOREOVER, soon after he took up the life of a monk did Luther face the disillusionment and discontent with his lifestyle and actions which sparked in his soul a yearning to look for a greater truth and higher purpose. It was this search for solace that would ultimately lead him to embrace the doctrines that he later coined in the realm of Christian theology.

LUTHER'S VIEW ON MARRIAGE
AND CELIBACY

❦

L uther absolutely ridiculed the concept of celibacy as being contradictory to the very nature of man who needed love and companionship, besides the hypocrisy of the Christian priests who were deep in immorality while wearing a garb of celibate, monastic life disgusted him. When Luther did decide to marry Catharina Von Bora who was just 26 while he was 41, it raised many eye brows. He received a lot of negative criticism even from people within the reformist movement. Particularly critical and apprehensive of this decision was Philipp Melanchthon who seemed to fear that her coming was an evil omen for the Protestant movement. This was despite the fact that many other priests had already married, among them being Andreas Karlstadt and Justus Jonas.

❦

IN FACT, like his other ideas, Luther's stance over the willingness to get married and the likelihood of taking a wife seems to have taken a sudden turn. In 1525, he had written a letter to George Spalatin saying that he would never take a wife given that he often lived like a fugitive and had so many other things to worry about. Amusingly, Luther seems to have genuinely fallen in love with the woman who seemed so much like himself; one who dreaded boredom and abhorred empty ritualism. In fact, it seems Luther's intuition about Katharine was right as she soon brought much needed order to his life and became the manager of his household and the handler of his finances.

LUTHER'S VIEW ON THE BIBLE

౷౷

L uther regarded the Bible not only as a tool to be used during Liturgy and worship but also as the prime source of law and legislation in the Christian religion. To him, all spirituality and theology must be unarguably based on the Bible and anything that contradicts the Bible cannot be claimed to be a genuine part of the Christian faith. Further, his immersion into Biblical study lead him to a profound realization; that salvation depended on faith and not deeds. It was God's grace and not the insignificant deeds of man that would save a man's soul from damnation.

LUTHER'S VIEWS ON THE CHURCH

৩⅍৩

I nitially, like any other Christian Luther respected the Church at Rome and showed reverence to the office of the Pope and his spiritual authority like any other Christian. However, coming from the Augustinian tradition, it didn't take him long to realize the disparity in the Catholic Church's treatment of priests and pastors from Germany. After a visit to Rome the internal corruptions of the Church became exposed to him and he realized that everything wasn't well at the heart of the Christian empire. Gradually as he delved deeper into theology and Biblical study he was convinced that the Church had strayed far away from what was actually taught by Christ as the right way of live and spirituality. Among the practices of the Church he found repugnant was the practice of offering indulgences whereby common men would buy their salvation against a sum of money. Luther criticized the Church for such materialism as well as other immoral and unjust practices.

෪෪෨

PARTICULARLY, the scandal of offering Indulgences came under direct fire from Luther. He denounced such a practice including Peter's Indulgence and criticized the whole idea of buying indulgences as it was almost akin to buying salvation. During Luther's time Johann Tetzel was a priest infamous for the sale of indulgences and supported the Papal court and Bishop Albrecht Von Brandenberg in this corrupt practice. To their displeasure Luther opposed their actions and this coveted way of extracting money from gullible masses and so he came under heavy criticism from these priests whose livelihood he had snatched. In response of this corruption when Luther wrote the *95 Theses,* legends spread that he had nailed the document to the door of the Wittenberg Castle Church. Which this was an exaggeration what he had actually done was to send it out to some Bishops and in the after-math, was surprised by their positive response.

෪෪෨

FURTHER, it must be remembered that while Luther's position against the Church was based on facts and firsthand experience, the ill treatment that the Church meted out to him seems to have stemmed from Historical events that even precede the birth of Luther. A s a matter of fact, the Church had always seen rebellions in Germany as a treat to its temporal and spiritual authority. The Hussite wars of 1468-1478 also knows as the Bohemian wars which were anti-pope in nature and gave the Roman empire a tough time as well as the Bundshuh movement od 1493-1517, which were a series of Peasant Rebellions, had already formed the Church's precon-ceived notion of simmering troubles within Germany which could boil over any day and engulf the empire within its flames. It therefore seems that the harshness and bitterness Church officials showed towards Luther was based on these past experiences although Luther never directly supported violence or rebellion in any form.

❦

THE PEAK of the Church's bitterness against Luther was when in 1518 an inquisition was started against Luther in Rome. Although things quietened a bit with emperor Maximillian's death, as soon as Karl V was king, matters worsened and soon Luther was treated as a rebel. It seems that Luther's 1517 comments in *95 Theses* about the Pope wherein he fearlessly and directly addressed the Pope, had not gone well with Rome. Immediately thereafter the Archbishop Albrecht had the *95 Theses* checked for heresy and sent to Rome since Pope Leo X's attitude was to deal with reformers carefully. Luther had been bold enough to question rather wittily as to why the Pope doesn't build the Basilica of St. Peter from his own enormous wealth. In response, he was summoned by the Imperial Diet of Augsburg in 1518.

❦

IN FACT, right from 1517 to 1520 an entire gang of papal theologians were tirelessly working against Luther. Their efforts at defaming Luther made the Pope declare in 1518 that Luther's teachings contradicted the Church and in 1520 he declared Luther a heretic with 120 days to recant. The roaring tiger that Luther was, he didn't relent and in 1521 he was excommunicated from the Catholic Church. When in March 1521 at the Diet of Worms Luther did not recant, in March the assembly declared Luther to be a convict and banned his writings. This forced Luther to go into hiding at the Wartburg castle while Charles V ordered his writings to be burnt. Even in 1522 Luther was in hiding in Eisenach, before he could finally return to public life. Thus, it was quite a bumpy ride for Luther with Catholic priests thirsty for his blood. It must have taken a lot of attitude to become a thorn in the foot of none other than the Vicar of God on Earth!

LUTHER'S DOCTRINE OF
JUSTIFICATION

꧁꧂

The culmination of Luther's study of the Bible and Christian theology a swell as his own deeply profound spiritual experiences and first-hand accounts of struggle with faith brought about a profound realization upon Luther- one that he expressed so eloquently in his doctrine of Justification, which he viewed as central to Christianity. According to Luther deeds are divorced from faith and a sinner can be declared righteous by God merely on the basis of his faith and that the righteousness of Christians stems from the righteousness of Christ through no merit or conscious effort on their own. In this Luther seems to agree with St. Paul that one's good deeds are mere filthy rags while salvation comes through divine grace.

꧁꧂

LUTHER OFTEN REPEATED the statement "Faith alone makes someone just and fulfills the law". Further, he articulated this doctrine very well in his Bondage of Will in 1525. Luther's position on predestination was mostly based on the Epistle of St Paul The Ephesians 2:8-10 while his position on righteousness was derived from Romans 1:17 which insists that the righteousness of man depends on his faith.

❧ VI ❧
LUTHER IN LATER
YEARS - LIFE AFTER 1525

❦

Prayer is a strong wall and fortress of the church; it is a goodly Christian weapon.
    Martin Luther

❦

While Luther was born in a Germany of infighting and confusion, little improved during his own lifetime. There were often wars and uprisings, mostly by landless people, against the dominant feudalistic system that controlled the lives of people in middle aged Europe in general and Germany in particular.

❦

While 1525 brought much joy to Luther's life on account of his marriage and shines out like a bookmark in the book of his life, this was also the time when Germany war on fire due to the peasant rebellions that took place at several places in Germany between 1524 and 1525. Interestingly, though Luther was always for the empowerment and education of the masses and denounced excesses on the peasants, he did not support these rebellions and instead denounced them and encouraged local rulers to bring such revolting peasants into submission. It was in this connection that Luther wrote *Against the Murderous, Thieving Hordes of Peasants* which, appeared in May 1525.

જ૨૭

In fact in 1526, a thin ray of hope shone forth for Luther and other leaders of the Protestant Reformation in the form of the Diet of Spyres which granted local rulers more powers and greater autonomy to the Protestant Reformation to decide about the nature of reforms in their Churches. However, this hope died out soon and the Church came down on the Protestants with a heavy hand.

A SERIES OF TRIALS AND
TRIBULATIONS (1531-1546)

꧁꧂

This part of Luther's life was perhaps the most tumultuous and stressful with all kinds of trials and tribulations coming his way. On one hand, his own health started failing him and he remained ill more often with problems affecting his eyes, ears, heart and kidneys. While he struggled with his health complications, the situation around him kept deteriorating. Notwithstanding the bitterness and opposition, he faced from the Catholic camp, even within the reformation there were splits among the reformers themselves. Thus, Luther had added responsibility as the leader to keep his flock together and arbitrate disputes among the followers. It is said that this was one reason why Luther kept going back on many of his ambitious projects like revamping the process of worship and liturgy among church goers since he needed to minimize changes that would split the masses or leaders of the reformation.

꧁꧂

ALSO, other major scandals taking place in Germany at the time that consumed much of Luther's time and energy included the Bigamy of Philip I, the Landgrave of Hesse. A peculiar character, Philip I had come into Luther's pail and become one of the sheep in his flock, which is why issues related to him became issues of Luther's concern. It was in 1521 Phillip I first met Luther and finally converted to protestant Christianity in 1524 at the hands of Melanchthon. While Philip's conversion had added much strength to the protestant reformation, given his status as a ruler, his personal affairs caused much public uproar as he tried to break social taboos. His intent to remarry while his first wife was still alive, popularly known as the scandal of the bigamy of Philip I created some friction even within the Protestant ranks. While Luther advised him against it saying that the example of the Old Testament patriarchs wasn't enough as a precedent in his case, Melanchthon encouraged him about it by saying that nothing in the divine injunctions forbade it for him. Since bigamy was a taboo in German Christian society, it became the talk of town for a long time until people found no time to engage in such discussions due to the years of subsequent war and violence.

❦

IN FACT, things only worsened towards the end of this period and conflicts increased in seriousness and size as Luther published the *Against the Papacy at Rome Founded by the Devil* in 1545 which was a very strong blow to the Roman Church and the empire that had been built on the foundation of Catholic religion. This point is regarded as the height of the Protestant Reformation and it was at this point that Luther and his supporters were most active and most feared. However, things only began worse as Luther gave his last sermon in

Eiselben in 1546 wherein he directly attacked the Jews and called for them to thrown out. So now Luther had only compounded his own troubles; on one hand, he had the Catholics after his blood and on the other the Jews were now his fierce enemies due to the hatred he had displayed against them in his fiery speeches.

❧ VII ❧

LUTHER'S BURDEN-CHALLENGING AND REFORMING THE CHURCH

❦

For in the true nature of things, if we rightly consider, every green tree is far more glorious than if it were made of gold and silver.

Martin Luther

❦

In stark contrast to all this, Luther's view of a new reformed church was one which makes personal faith primary and confession of sin and personal experience the bedrock of religious experience. He also insisted that local Churches must be inclusive to the local population.

❦

An important aspect of Luther's attempt to reform the Christian Church was the strengthening of local Churches in Germany and empowering them to maintain a certain degree of independence from the Catholic bastion at Rome. This was important in his sight to effectively safeguard the Protestant Reformation and for it to gain stronghold in Germany. Without first establishing itself in one geographical area the movement would have died out in its infancy.

۞

Within Germany Luther took a number of measures to implement his reformed ideas among Church communities. In order to ensure that the reformers who spearheaded the revolution were genuinely taken care of, Luther made sure that local pastors were ensure a steady salary so that the reformation did not suffer in any way due to the domestic problems of the priests. Then again, a major aspect was Church service reform wherein Luther fought for allowing local parish to take part of the wafer and the wine during holy communion. This was the beginning of his image as a man of the masses.

۞

Moreover, having witnessed widespread corruption and decadence within the Catholic Church, Luther travelled far and wide in order to ensure that reform efforts were going on in the way they should. Also, he realized the need for accountability and transparency and so he travelled a lot just to keep a check on pastors appointed by him. Many" of Luther's dictates on how work within the Church was to take place was summarized in a document, *Instruction on the Visitations to*

Pastors in the Electorate of Saxon, which was written by Philipp Melanchthon in 1528.

❦

Luther concentrated all his efforts on the establishment of a central council that would overlook the working of the Church, supervise functioning and would be able to keep everything under check. Between 1515 and 1529 Luther worked tirelessly to establish the Supervisory Council for the Church. The Church at Saxony would function in an advisory capacity which Churches in other provinces under its leadership.

❦

Also, since Luther realized that his reform efforts would require him to secure alternative source of funding as the Roman Church would no longer spend money on churches under the reformers. As a result, Luther struck alliances with various political factions such as secular German princes. Also, during this time Luther came in close contact with John the Steadfast who was a government official in Saxony. This man helped Luther by providing the necessary money and leadership because the break up with Rome had had a negative effect on the German government's finances as well. However not everyone liked the idea of such an alliance. Some even criticize such an alliance and blame it for giving rise to the form of Church Government that came into existence subsequently.

❧ VIII ☙

IMPORTANT WORKS AND CONTRIBUTIONS

❧❦❧

Pray, and let God worry.
Martin Luther

❧❦❧

The writings of Martin Luther span volumes of well written and often argumentative works in the forms of books, articles and even pamphlets. One factor that greatly aided him in his endeavor to circulate his writings and aid the cause of the Protestant Reformation among commoners and nobles alike seems to have been the availability of the Guttenberg press. It is often remarked that his writings formed a fifth of whatever was printed in Germany during the prime years of the revolution.

Undoubtedly, Martin Luther's magnum opus remains his translation of the Bible into German. It was in 1522 that Luther published his translation of the New Testament and later he completed the translation of the entire Bible while he was imprisoned in Coburg in 1530. Finally, in 1534 Luther published the complete translation of the Bible in the Saxony variant of German that was popular in Northern and Southern parts and could be understood by Germans from all over the nation. In fact. Luther kept revising and refining his translation right until his death, with the sole intention of providing the common man a person access to the Bible without any hindrance or interference by authority figures within the Church.

❧

While Luther also used the translation of the Bible to advance his doctrine, it had numerous positive effects on the empowerment of common Christians viz a viz their faith and religious principles. It ensured that masses would not be beguiled by Priests who doled out passages of the Bible at will and kept the public's access to religious knowledge under strict check. Also, the mastery of language and rhetoric in this work of Luther influenced German language and literature in the 15th and 16th century and paved the way for a series of translation culminating in that of Tyndall and the King James Version. Also, the comic side of Luther's genius shone through the pages of his German Bible as he instructed Lucas Lanarch to draw imagery discrediting the pope within its pages. The public was amused by this novelty and it helped arouse not only curiosity but also spread the Protestant doctrine. Thus, Protestantism gained popularity due to the pent-up feelings within the public against the Pope that it succeeded at reigniting.

৩৵৩

Moreover, Luther wrote widely in the areas of Theology, salvation, Belief and Faith. His famous work *The Bondage of the Will* is regarded as the masterpiece of the Protestant reformation. Luther wrote this treatise in response to *The Diatribe of Freewill* written by Desirius Erasmus. Also, his 1917 publication *95 Theses* or *Disputation on The Power and Efficacy of Indulgences* which laid down the doctrine of Justification and salvation through God's grace alone sough to separate human faith from human actions, emphasizing the former over the later. Moreover the 95 theses clearly summarized faith into two catechisms and served a death blow to the Church by challenging the Pope's office on one hand and also ridiculing the practice of issuing Indulgences on the other.

৩৵৩

Moreover, Luther also wrote about the happenings that took place around him as well as more direct criticism of the Church itself. In 1525 Luther wrote *Against the Murderous, Thieving Hordes of Peasants* in reference to the peasant wars in Germany and in 1454 Luther published *Against the Papacy at Rome Founded by the Devil.*

৩৵৩

Also, Luther delved into the issues that involved other Christian sects and neighboring religions such as Judaism. Particularly with the Jews he had a sweet-sour relationship which ranged from welcoming them with open arms to calling for their expulsion from Germany. In 1523 Luther wrote *Jesus was born a Jew* while two decades later in 1543 he wrote *Jews and their Lies*, which was to later earn him criticism for anti-Semitic remarks.

❧ IX ❧

DEATH AND LEGACY OF LUTHER

❧❧❧

Our Lord has written the promise of resurrection, not in books alone, but in every leaf in springtime.
   Martin Luther

❧❧❧

On the 18th of February 1546, Luther passed away in his hometown in Eisleben and was laid to rest in Castle Church on 22nd February. With his death, a momentous era in Christian history had come to an end; an era of great confusion but also great promise- a promise of a better future, a more enlightened and reformed Church community that could focus their thoughts and action on God and his love instead of focusing on materialism and worldly gains.

❧

Luther was an extremely influential person when he was alive and even after his death. After all his writings sparked the Protestant reformation, his efforts lead to common masses having access to the Holy Bible in their native tongues, his ideas split the Roman Catholic Church and he forever changed the way Christian Theology was viewed and taught. To have achieved all that in one lifetime isn't an ordinary task. It speaks of the greatness of Luther's ambition and the genius of his though.

❧

The prolific writer that he was, Luther was also very wise at using all resources at his disposal and so he made judicious use of the Guttenberg press. In fact, it is often estimated that one fifth of all material printed at the press between 1500 and 1530 consisted of Luther's writings. Also, the genius that Luther was, his public perception had been positively molded by a selective use of printed images of himself that appeared alongside his written works. These images helped re-create Luther in a hero's image among the German public as his artists did a wonderful job with giving him a strong face and large built that immediately made him resemble the princes of Germany. In comparison to Luther most Christian saints and priests appeared insignificant and weak while he looked more like a Greek god. In this manner Luther became the face of the protestant revolution in Germany and people preferred identifying with a man who was strong and healthy and cared to defend the masses against the onslaught of Church clergy.

❧

As is with most great thinkers and philosophers, the work of this great revolutionary did not bear fruit during his lifetime, but rather hundreds of years later. While Luther was ridiculed and mock by his adversaries and opponents in Christian circles during his own lifetime, it was only decades and centuries later that the Christian world could open its eyes to the reality of what he was hoping to convey through his distinct theology.

⚜

It was only in 1999 that a Joint Declaration on the Doctrine of Justification (JDDJ) was jointly accepted by both the Catholic Church's Pontifical Council for Promoting Christian Unity (PCPCU) and the Lutheran World Federation. Finally decades of ecumenical dialogue and peace building measures had ended centuries of hostility and joined all main Christian denominations upon what Luther had ventured out to revive of the doctrine of salvation through Christ. The JDDJ declared that all Churches have now reached common ground regarding justification by God's grace through faith in Christ. Almost a decade later, in July 2006, the World Methodist Council adopted the same declaration and continued the legacy of Luther. Finally, only recently in 2017, The World Communion of Reformed Churches (Congregational, Presbyterian, Reformed, United, Uniting, and Waldensian), followed suit and also adopted the declaration.

⚜

Thus, in a spirit of arbitration and mutual understanding that Luther would have loved to see during his own lifetime, Christian denominations have all come to accept the Doctrine of Justification with very minimal disagreements and finally instead of being a divisive force, Luther's Theology has finally sought to united disunited factions of the faith that he so dearly sought to preserve. One aspect of Luther's legacy is that he set Christian thinkers seriously reconsidering many aspects of belief and stirred Christian activists into serious action which ultimately lead into the further formation of several Christian reformist groups. Luther's thought influenced an extensive list of movements and ideas main among them being Protestantism, Lutheranism, Anglicanism and the Reformed tradition. While Protestants do not condemn him in any way, some other traditions hold him in greater reverence than other reformers and thinkers.

৩১৯

In view of his innumerable sacrifices for restoring the Christian faith to its pristine glory and purity and ensuring that the masses are not beguiled in the name of salvation and deliverance, Luther is remembered on the 18th of February in the Lutheran and the Episcopal calendar of Saints and the Church of England Celebrates his contributions on the 31st of October each year. Further, Reformation Day specifically commemorates the writing of the 95 Theses. Moreover, a number of places in Germany bear his name such as Lutherstadt Eisleben, Lutherstadt Willenberg and Mansfeld Lutherstadt.

LUTHER UP CLOSE-HIS PERSONALITY AND TRAITS

Next to the Word of God, the noble art of music is the greatest treasure in the world.

Martin Luther

Although unravelling the personality of Luther, one of the most complicated and sophisticated Christian thinkers, is no easy task, some of the most striking qualities about him include his ability to think out of the box, his linguistic and logical reasoning abilities, his effective public speaking and leadership skills, his dedicating to the love of God, his loyalty to his comrades, his fearless bravery in front of the mighty Roman empire and Church, his passion to bring the truth to light, his love for the masses and keenness to liberate them from slavery and religious manipulation, his joyous and humorous nature, his deep love and devotion to his wife and children. At the same time, humorous contrasts to these qualities include his total failure to cope up with the horrendous life of a monk, his great displeasure at rote learning and intellectual slavery at school and university and his poor management skills at home which often left his surroundings in a total mess- something that his wife later took in her own hands and did a much better job at!

PERSONALITY

※

U ndoubtedly, of the traits that stand out in Luther's works and career are: his insistence on testing and experimenting with supposedly established facts to check for their veracity and the zeal to experience things first hand which other people merely took for granted. A gift from his great teachers these two lessons invariably created some profound results in his personality. Firstly, he learned to question authority and challenge anything that defies sound reasoning. Secondly, he refused to accept anything without testing it out and experiencing it for himself. Perhaps these two traits made him the formidable mad that the Church so feared for these two traits were what had been brushed under the carpet though centuries of oppression and intellectual degradation of common masses in Europe.

※

Moreover, what's particularly remarkable is Luther's ability to just be himself and not lose his identity or personality despite the taxing responsibilities that came upon his shoulders as a spokesman for Christianity, leader of the protestant reformation and a religious thinker. Nevertheless, he managed to be himself and his passion for enjoying the gifts of life shone through at several intervals of his life such as his decision to marry and his refusal to accept celibacy. Further, his love for the arts and fine music which he encouraged to be used generously in worship and service, also points towards his pleasant and fun-loving nature. He even became an eye sore for the extremely religious and orthodox as he neither shunned away drinking nor indulgence in worldly pleasures.

Luther was therefore, no moral giant as he accepted the shortcomings of human nature and allowed worldly indulgences to a far greater extent than his Catholic coreligionists. Unquestionably this allowance seems to be related to his theology of justification. Luther firmly believed that God doesn't look at what people did but that he looked at the faith in one's heart. However, adversaries who failed to recognize the value of his ideas, blamed him for attempting to spread licentiousness and immorality within the churches of Germany.

From what is evident about his education and career he always seemed to follow his heart over his mind. One can easily recall how he decided to change his career from law to theology based on the fact that his heart didn't find satisfaction in the former. The incident of the snowstorm perhaps only worked to seal that decision which heart had already taken. In other words, Luther remained unhappy in anything that he was made to do against his will or personality.

༺༻

MOREOVER, with that being sad Luther was no machine. He had emotions and he often expressed them very openly. His anger was just as fierce as his love and devotion to knowing God and his love for the masses whom he wanted to save from the slavery of the Church. At several instances during his career he ends up picking fights and inciting violence, although he always condemned the use of violence especially between sects of the Christian faith. One famous incident where Luther had an angry exchange of words was at the Imperial Diet in Augusburg in 1518, where he had been summoned to defend the accusations regarding heresy. Instead of trying to save his neck, Luther stuck to his principles and had a heated exchange with Cardinal Thomas Cajetan. Their arguments lasted for three days, at the end of which they had a full-blown shouting match that infuriated the Cardinal to an extent that Luther had to escape while the Pope declared his writings to be contradictory to Church teachings.

༺༻

SO YES, funnily, our hero did have an anger problem and he never shied away from expressing his emotions effectively. Perhaps some would say that he would have been better of just if knew how to control his anger and express his emotions more wisely. However, as we said earlier, Luther wasn't a fake public figure; he was who he was and his attitude changed for no man, not even the pope.

❧

SOMETIMES, Luther's tendency to voice his passions did take a negative turn although he might not have intended so. Particularly with regard to non-Christian religions he won himself a bad reputation. His fiery speeches against the Jews as well as Muslims were often regarded as untimely and unneeded since the Christian world was already dealing with so much. It was due to his utterances about the Jews and his writings against them in particular that he is sometimes blamed for antisemitism.

❧

IN FACT, Luther's criticism of Jewish practices and what he saw as their ploy to take control of society at the cost of Christian masses, has been interpreted as some historians as the precursor to full blown anti-Semitism in his homeland. Many look at his writings such as the 1543 document "Jews and their lies" and trace the roots of German anti-Semitism, that was later used by the Nazi party to orchestrate the holocaust, back to Luther. How far this claim is true remains debatable as it was never Luther's primary interest to cause any physical harm to the Jews and secondly, he never maintained a singular stance about them throughout his career. For instance, he had previously published Jesus was born a Jew in 1523 which was a strike contrast. Again, as we said it is impossible to fully understand Luther and this is a classic example of bewilderment at how aspects of his personality and his works appear to be contradictory and leave the reader confused and guessing. A similar sort of confusion arises if one were to read the document that Melanchthon wrote in 1528. Interestingly, Luther approved this document despite the fact that it stresses on repentance repeatedly, whereas, Luther insisted that deeds were insignificant and justification through God's grace alone brings salvation.

༺✦༻

SURPRISINGLY, one would be taken aback to find that despite his apparent flaws and volatile temper, Luther was actually a genuine arbitrator and had some mastery at solving disputes. Perhaps it was his ability to analyze issues logically and go to the heart of the matter that enabled him to objectively understand disputes while his uncanny defense of the truth against all odds made people trust his sense of justice and good judgement. One of the most profound examples of his ability to arbitrate disputes took place at the very end of his life. ARBITRATION

༺✦༻

MOREOVER, his emotions never really interfered with his plans and his maneuver for the political establishment of the protestant reformation. The resourceful man that he was, he grabbed every opportunity that he found to strengthen the foundations of the reformation and ensured that the people who had appointed him as a leader would not be left helpless. He therefore saw it wise to rally with some secular German princes; who did not see it fit to over-emphasize religion with regard to German nationhood, nor indulged in matters concerning the beliefs of the citizens; against the Roman Catholic Church which was causing a problem to the princes just as it was oppressing the masses. By taking this politically brave decision Luther was able to garner some protection for his followers against anticipated attacks by Catholics.

❦

As several facets of his personality come to light across the span of his life, we see that this fun-loving man who was often fearlessly lazy enough to allow fungus to develop on his bedding and poor manager of the household that he was, was extremely patient in the face of disease and hardships. He accepted the hardships that God placed in his life with a smile, never once losing his faith or trust in God's grace- an ideal he sought to re-instill in Christianity. Thus, we see that he faced many diseases in his later years particularly around 1536 to 1544; heart problems, ear infections, Meniere's, fainting spells, cataract infections as well as stone sin the kidney and gall bladder; which made it difficult to work normally but continued to serve the masses and teach at university until his last days on this Earth.

❦

Luther was therefore unquestionably resilient and brave, an able educationist and great teacher, a visionary and a true leader. The funny thing about him being that no matter how much of a deep thinker and philosopher he seems at the surface, he was a fun-loving person and got bored very easily. In fact, he dreaded boredom to such an extent that the grammar schools he went to in his early years were no less than hell for him. Perhaps his hatred for those boring and miserable schools where they literally tortured children into rote memorization is only comparable to his utter dislike for the lifeless and soul sucking practices that he had to undergo as a monk. He often remarked how the monotonous routine and the obsessively repeatedly meaningless outer actions left him sick at heart and yearning for a spiritual rescue to come from God himself. Ironically, so much did Luther hate boredom that even in devotion and worship he always needed some joy and lighter moments to keep his spirits alive. Perhaps this quality is what set him so apart from his colleagues and made him appear as a threat to the status quo that had been maintained by most Church officials towards useless norms and taboos of the Roman Catholic tradition.

PERSONAL AND FAMILY LIFE

৩৯৫

Recognizing the follies and shortcomings of human nature, Luther faced the truth and refused to accept unlike most priests of the day that celibacy was a way to get closer to God. Instead he argued that the Bible never recommended it. He therefore took a wife in 1525, Katharina Von Bora, and started the life of a householder. From what his family and friends must say about him he was a loving husband, father and dutiful uncle. This family man was no misogynist and instead saw woman as a partner in man's life and achievements. Under his care his wife flourished and continued to play her natural role in the Christian community around her. In fact, Luther was very attached to his six children and loved them so deeply that when he lost his daughter Magdalena in 1542, it caused him great distress and sadness. Some would say that he wasn't the same person thereafter as the loss affected his emotionally as well as physically and psychologically.

LUTHER'S HOME was a full house and mostly a mess because of being overcrowded, but, that also indicated that he had a big heart. His shabby cramped home housed not only his own family of 8 but six of his sister's children and one of his wife's relatives. However, his generosity extended beyond that and when his students needed a place to stay he rented out parts of his own home to them. That surely made the place even more over crowded but the rent the students paid was a welcome addition to the family's meagre income.

ANOTHER AMUSING ASPECT of Luther's personal life was that he and his wife Katharina were an almost comical couple, with both having tried the life of a Christian and hermit and both having been miserably let down by the nature of monastic life at their time. On one hand, we have Luther who almost fell ill due to the dire hardships and unnatural ways of monastic life and its demands and on the other hand we have Katharina- who escaped the convent at Nimbsch after having an equally bitter experience. Ironically, like two fugitives from war, they found in each other the love and peace that they had longed for. In fact, contrary to the predictions of some reformists, the coming of this woman in Luther's life did not take him away from God or his responsibilities as the leader of the revolution but instead added fuel to the fire and further armed him to fight more valiantly against injustice and excesses of the Church.

❧ XI ❧

CONCLUSION

❦

Faith is a living, daring confidence in God's grace, so sure and certain that a man could stake his life on it a thousand times.

Martin Luther

❦

In an era of violence and bloodshed, where religion had failed Europe in providing either succor to the masses or meaning to the lives of the affluent, and where faith in Christ was used as a tool for money making and priests abused their power to beguile commoners, a clarion call was sounded to denounce such treachery and falsehood. The protestant reformation took birth with one man as its father and master planner: Martin Luther.

Luther- the monk, the priest, the reformer, the loving father, the brave soldier, the generous brother and the man of the common man in Germany rose to face a mighty empire which was hiding its imperialism behind the garb of religion; using the office of the Pope and the Catholic church as a shield to subjugate the mind of common Christians. Against this hypocrisy Luther stood up and fought valiantly, losing his health, wealth and peace of mind. However, none of his efforts were in vain. After his death in 1555 the Roman empire and Catholic church were forced to accept Protestantism as a legitimate faith.

❧

Undoubtedly, most of the freedoms that common Christians enjoy, like the ability to read the Bible in their own tongues, the liberty to organize local Churches, partake the wafer and wine during Holy Communion and the very right to live a life of personalized faith in God the benevolent without being harassed or enslaved by a Church are all blessings that stemmed out of Luther's thought and which would have never been possible without him.

❧

With all his shortcomings and reservations, Luther brought new life to a dying spiritual tradition and rescued Christianity from the darkness of materialism and immorality. Criticized as he may be, he never sanctioned the violence that some practiced in his name and always distinguished between moral action and injustice. Luther was no pacifist, but neither was he a warmonger. He was who he was, and no one could force him to behave against his will and desire.

৯২৯

In conclusion, what can be said is that Luther was not a mere episode in the history of Christianity. He was the storm that brought down centuries of corruption and tyranny and set the tone for greater compassion, tolerance, dialogue and deeper introspection. The movement of reform started by him was a culmination of genuine anger and remorse and gave vent to the voice of the ordinary Christian. While Luther has passed into human memory, his spirit of enquiry lives on and gives hope to many more great thinkers and reformers who continue to make the world a better place.

❧ XII ❧
BEING LIKE LUTHER-INSPIRATIONAL QUOTES AND ACTIONABLE TIPS

෨෨෨

Displaying Courage

෨෨෨

One of the most profound lessons we learn from Luther is to show bravery and courage even in front of a strong adversary. Much like the story of David and Goliath from the Bible, we learn from Luther's life how an ordinary man with extraordinary ideas by the dint of his will can challenge an entire empire disguised as the Christian Church and bring down the façade to reveal its real picture.

In our own lives, we are often faced by tyrants in the form of people or institutions that treat us or those around us unjustly. Whether it is racism, sexism, judicial disparity or even harassment at the workplace, we can follow this great man by standing up for truth without caring for how powerful our enemy is.

⚜

Sticking to Your Principles

⚜

Again, just as Luther refused to bow down to pressure and instead maintained his staunch criticism of actions that went against his principles of justice and honesty, we too must stick to our principles even in the face of hardships that we might face in the process.

⚜

Questioning Authority

⚜

While we often tend to be carried into the flow of the stream, we need to pause at brief intervals and question the legitimacy of those in authority. Whether it is the ruler of the country, our local ministers or our bosses at work, Luther teaches us to keep our eyes open for anything that goes against our convictions or even common sense. Whenever an authority figure sanctions something that is morally wrong, we must take it as our duty to speak out and question such policies.

❦

Rejecting Blind Faith

❦

This was something that Luther did all his life as he realized that blind faith only leads to greater ignorance. While it might be easier to achieve a high level of dogmatic conviction by choosing to surrender our faculty of reasoning, blind faith takes one nowhere. Instead, one must use our human capabilities of logical reasoning where ever possible to arrive at the pristine truth.

❦

Always Following Your Heart

❦

Having been always keen to follow his heart, no matter how much it kept on wavering, Luther realized early on that one can do best in life only by being true to one's inner calling. Likewise, we should never be troubled or discouraged by well-meaning criticism of people around us, and instead keep following our heart to do what we are genuinely passionate about.

❦

Keeping Life Fun-filled

❦

The great thinker and reformer that Luther was, he is set apart from his colleagues by the single trait that he gave enough time to recreation and having fun in the right measure. In order to avoid boredom or monotony, taking time to simply unwind can be a great boost in our daily routines. Keeping worship alive with positive indulgences and innovative ways e.g. Music was something Luther practiced and preached. This is best illustrated by his saying: "He who sings prays double".

৩৯৩

Focusing On God's Grace And Not On One's Follies

৩৯৩

Something that Luther learnt early on after taking up monastic life, if one tends to over emphasize human follies and weakness it can only lead to depression and sorrow. Instead, to maintain a positive frame of mind what we must do instead is to ponder over life's immense beauty and the infinite gifts we enjoy each day as human beings and the unending Divine Grace of God that encompasses all things with mercy and compassion. The resultant positivity will help us jet speed ahead at full steam.

৩৯৩

Standing Up For The Weak And Oppressed

৩৯৩

While other religious figures rallied with powerful monarchs, Luther chose to voice the concerns of the weak and oppressed in society and the masses that were weak and powerless. While it might be tempting to please those in power, we must make it a common practice to at least speak out about the rights of those who are less fortunate and make sure they have a voice.

⚜

Being Resourceful And Gathering Strength

⚜

One of the amazing lessons from Luther's life is his resourcefulness and his ability to rally people for his cause. In doing so Luther used all material and human resources at his disposal and even allied with secular German princes for the advancement of the Protestant reformation. On one hand, he printed literature and had it distributed to create awareness about his mission, on the other hand he garnered support from those in positions of power and worked hard to ensure that his men were safe from Catholic attacks and had proper salaries to maintain their families. All of this teaches us that we must not put all our eggs in the same basket but instead diversify our approach and ensure that we increase our strength in all aspects in order to achieve our goals.

⚜

Looking Out For Your Team Mates And People Under Your Care

❧

Perhaps this is one of the things that Luther did best. Not only was he very loyal to his family and chose to take care of sister's children, he was also a dutiful husband and caring father. In his professional life, he showed similar interest in the lives of his students and ensured that they had what they needed. Moreover, as someone spearheading the protestant movement, he always stood with his comrades. Luther went to great lengths to ensure all the Protestant priests had fixed salaries and that they were not harassed or punished by the Catholic Church. Similarly, he also stood up to protect and shield all those who had converted to his cause, like in the issue of the landgrave of Hesse.

❧

The lesson we can learn from this is to always display our loyalty and support to people who are loyal to us. In a short life, what we really need to do is to value people. To cherish and treasure our family and friends, and to stand up to offer support to people we have worked with- those are the real values which can help us make the world a better place and leave a legacy much like Martin Luther.

❧ XIII ☙

FURTHER READING ON LUTHER

❧☙

Naturally, Luther's life is not the life of any ordinary man; it is thrilling, intriguing, amusing, romantic, funny, comical and tragic all at the same time. Someone who would like to be recommended further reading on Martin Luther can refer to these three works:

- Luther the Reformer: The Story of the Man and His Career by James M. Kittelson
- Here I Stand: A Life of Martin Luther by Roland Bainton
- Luther: Man Between God and the Devil by Heiko Oberman

❧☙

While Kittelson seeks to trace the development of Luther as a reformer and revolutionary, stopping to analyze the trajectory of his career and works, Baiton's analysis is a more passionate analysis of his life as a man of conscience and believer in Christ. Oberman takes a slightly different take on Luther and offers insights into his struggles, crises of faith, his deliverance from error and his rediscovery of the essence of faith, salvation and justification by god's grace.

⚜

For someone interested in Luther's concept of God and his unique theological standpoints such as salvation by justification and centrality of confessions, the work of Paul Althaus, *The theology of Martin Luther,* is an excellent reference. The book not only discusses how Luther's theology stems from the Bible itself but also explains its most salient features and how it differed from the theology of the Catholic church. Furthermore, the implications of such a theology on life and works of a Christian believer are also discussed to some extent.

YOUR FREE EBOOK!

As a way of saying thank you for reading our book, we're offering you a free copy of the below eBook.

Happy Reading!

23777924R00059

Made in the USA
Columbia, SC
13 August 2018